What others are saying about this book:

Finally there is a book that offers more than speculation. Through the eye and thoughts of the poet, we are invited to "Come Inside." Small town America where the mind is troubled and relaxed: the body is shaken and soothed and the spirit is set free. Deborah Tillman is a midwife of poetry. May she continue to birth in abundance.
> **—Lois Dabney Smith, P.H.D.**
> **Nationally recognized Psychotherapist**

Thank you for the invitation to "Come Inside". The life lessons you've shared are relevant to God's children of all ages—young and old. Taking a trip down memory lane, being challenged by societal norms or reflecting with your personal insights—this book speaks to the heart.
> **—Crystal L. Gunn Tucker, P.H.D.**
> **Taylor Allderdice High**

Sho–Nuff is how I describe Deborah's book of poetry "Come Inside". It was a fantastic journey involving love, reality, and spirituality to spare. It is now a valued part of my library. Again Sho–Nuff.
> **—Moses Shabaka**
> **Operator–Port Authority of Allegheny County**

I enjoyed reading this book a reflection of life. A journey through love, joy, pain, and happiness. Something for the young to enjoy and understand. Thank you Deborah!!
> **—Tina Solomon**
> **student–Duquesne University**

After reading your book, I'm impressed with your talent and skills. And I am proud to be from the "old" Duquesne, which had the morals and values you described, and that you described so perfectly.
> **—Pastor Perrin**
> **Macedonia Baptist Church–Duquesne, PA**

Having been born and raised in small town Duquesne, PA "Come Inside", was a trip back in time, hollowed and longed for; into the present, wondering how did it change so much; and through the author's eyes, looking to the future, by using the past to move through the present, elegantly building a future, one that is filled with love, hope, and spirituality. I believe the future does hold hope for better days.
> **—D___on Lennon**
> **___nia Baptist Church–Duquesne, PA**

D0423565

Come Inside

Poetry from one heart

Deborah Lindsay Tillman

Original Edition

HPC Harobed Publishing Creations, Pittsburgh, PA

Come Inside
Poetry from one heart

By Deborah Lindsay Tillman

Published by:
HPC Harobed Publishing Creations
Post Office Box 8195 Pittsburgh, PA 15217-0195

First printing 2003

Cover and book design by Robert Howard
Printed by Central Plains Book Manufacturing
Printed in the U.S.A.

Lindsay Tillman, Deborah
ISBN: 0-9679598-3-7
LCCN: 00-90093

Table of Contents

About the Author

Deborah started writing and drawing at the age of eight. Attended and became a member of *The Homewood Poetry Forum* in 1974. Started poetry recitals and short plays performing with the Forum progressing onward performing with *Three Shades of Mind: Belva Odom Salik & Brenda Odom Young.* Continued performing with the group for several years in events throughout the City of Pittsburgh and surrounding areas. Advanced on becoming a freelance writer, artist, and author. Member of various prestigious organizations, self-published and author of **Not Just Any Woman & Ode to Life.**

Dedicated

To GOD who made this possible.

My nephew Tiawon who believed I could.

Acknowledgement

For this book's preparation many friends and sources were consulted. Public resources, libraries, and departments of government.

Thank you for the beginning of this journey and those whom were with me throughout this process enabling me to share my works with others.

Cora Prince, Ernest Martin, Vickie & Charles Powell, Brenda Odom Young, Belva Odom Salik, Leah Young, Carol Ellis, Ardelle Robinson, Frank Hightower, Camille Sledd, Cynthia Conley, Don Mulberry, Winfred Coachman, John Brewer, Jothan Collins, Lavita Williams, Lettie Shaw, Nathan Davis, Linwood Salik, Malaya Rucker, Margie Gilcrese, Majorie Franklin, Mary Savage, Paulett Jones, Mujah Hameen, Ron Suber, Ron Porter, Sadie Anderson, Rob Penny, Amir, Akbar, and Syville Tidwell Woods.

Warning –Disclaimer

The purpose of this works is to guide you through another's life. Readers are selective of preference of what they choose to read. Making sense of the world through the thoughts and eyes of the poet, author.

The Author nor Harobed Publishing Creations shall have neither liability nor responsibility to an entity or person with the respect to any damage or loss caused, or alleged to be caused, directly or Indirectly by the contents of this book.

If you do not wish to be bound by the above, you may return this book to the publisher. You must send the original receipt or copy for full refund.

Introduction

Seven in the morning my PapPap and I would climb the hill across the street from our house. The Duquesne Steel Mill with its monstrous machines outlined the sky. PapPap and I would journey every morning with hoe, rake, giant sticks, and picks. On top of the hill laid flat unattended land miles long. Weeds sprouting from every direction popping their heads up from the tall trees baring different varieties of fruit. PapPap would stop place his tools upon the ground gaze upon the weeded field lean towards me and whisper in my ear, "One day you will become keeper of the land in a different way". I was six years old.

Six years later lying next to my great great grandmother who was asleep a bright aureole of light filled the room. Colors of burnt orange and yellow reminding me of fire's flame without the heat surrounded the room so bright making it difficult to watch. A reverent voice from within the center of the light spoke to me. "You are a blessed child". Slowly the light with its vibrant colors dispersed and vanished.

Filled with inner joy and excitement I awaken my great great grandmother. She listen as I explained what happened snuggled me close to her and stated, "My child you had a spiritual visitation from a Angel of GOD". Never once did she question me in regards to what I seen. At age thirteen she sent me to visit PapPap's son Pastor Ray Smith in Saginaw Michigan so he could explain to me what I had experience. I stayed with the pastor for two weeks visiting family, friends, and other pastors. Returning home assured I had witness a spiritual visitation from GOD.

Duquesne is a small town where everyone knew everyone. On cold winter nights my great great grandmother and I would hover around that big potbelly stove reading the Bible and singing spiritual hymns. Baptized by pastor Torrey a truly God-filled pastor in Macedonia Baptist Church. Filled with the elderly and young with voices that made your soul rumble.

From this small countrified city many talented people have come and Duquesne is a place I can always return. I am truly blessed and very thankful for the life I have been allowed to express.

Please Come Inside.........

Spirits Free

I Surrender Lord

Seized in the world's confusion,
Passing roads of corruption, grief, and pain.
This is not the life I need to live.
This is not what I'm to gain.
Tears shed, words unheard, left alone.
With a superficial soul with no destiny.
I surrender LORD.
I surrender unto you, to cleanse me,
Guide me, teach me, chestise me, and love me.
Fill me with your grace,
Place me on your throne of faith.
I surrender.
Discipline my life turn away deception,
Rid me of the fear inside.
Come quickly fill my mind and heart with wisdom.
Your love to praise throughout my everyday.
I surrender to you LORD,
And eternal life.

The Poet Messenger

Call me a troubadour.
Through others eyes an interpreter of visions, messenger.

The liberation, escape, reservations,
Rescues are the makeup of the troubadour,
The interpreter, the messenger,
Sonnets sung and spoken brought to listening ears.
Many styles, personalities, all with their own uniqueness.

Coating the world with beauty, sorrow, joy love and pain.
Painting life through different perspectives, dreams, visions,
Into gifts of individual foresight.
Peering through the windows of their heart.
Sharing a piece of their life.
I'm grateful to be.

One Moment In Time

Resisting heart weakened with no escape.
Cries piercing the dark words unheeded.
Fell into silent sleep awakened by desolation,
And despair.
Lack of convictions with no one to inveigh,
Self-abasement and shame.
Fortune and fame a game.
Shining knighthood to reign on a lonely throne.
Through the valleys of humiliation and stress,
Sickness near death.
Given a spurt of Heavenly Breath,
A reminder of that One moment in time.

Why?

Faultless bloodshed sees red.
Some mother, sister, father, brother, friend,
Has not slept.
        Destruction, violation more pain.
        Our youth deranged no remorse or shame.
Feel the rains pouring from their eyes.
Why?
Unknown bloodshed sees red.
Facades uncovered many faces all races.
Truth laid bare,
Youth's lost will neglected short-winded but real.

Some father, brother, sister, mother, friend,
Lay dead innocent bloodshed sees red.
Another cry to what end and Why?

Crying During The Night

I hear a child's cry during the night.
No one to console them nothing to eat no sleep,
Some left unattended wondering in the streets.

I hear a mother's cry during the night.
Beaten by the man she loves,
Some survive others died.

I hear a young girl's cry during the night.
Pregnant scared worn and torn.
Adulthood before childhood was born.

I hear a young boy's cry during the night.
To keep his dignity his pride he must fight,
Or innocently wiped out by a drive-bye.

I hear a father's cry during the night.
Lifetime of pain proving he's sane.
Stripped of his livelihood by societies games,
Facades, shame, and fame.
Manhood belittled living becoming a maze,
Of a price too high to pay.
A mans' world some say.
Seems as if there's no better way,
Hoping soon there will be light to shine,
Upon this darkened situation.

Remember

Remember when you could hang out all night long?
Sitting on your porch, your neighbor's, in the park, dark.
Favorite hang out spot.
Remember when fistfights were fights?
Play'n the dozen down play'n a cousin.
When music put fire in your feet sweat to your brow.
Grinds in your hips leaning to the ground.
Remember when catcher's kiss, double dutch,
Hopscotch, hide'n go seek, blind's man bluff, and midnight sneaks,
Were fun and games you were either with it or lame?
Well things aren't the same.
Now your doors are locked fistfights are replaced by drive-byes.
Music loud some too nasty to bare.
Well things are not the same people change,
Only remembrance of a time once lived.

A Dream A Vision

Three hundred years or more we slept,
Through the proverty that still remains,
Everything is not the same.
Secretes once being kept now being told,
Saying it is okay to deprive lives this way.
The land of the free integrated segregated as it be.
Wake up America let it be known,
Pollution, confusion, violence, pain, acid rain.
Power seekers to load in the richness of gain.
Stripping us of the land we build,
As they sit in high places playing racial games.
Of their free will to rob yes kill steal.
Wake up America let it be known that danger is at hand,
Our youth surrendering to dope loosing hope.
Caught up in wars, crime, doing time.
Being cool bringing guns to schools,
Dying.
America we've slept too long not to act to this destruction.

Color

We live in a society placarded by the color of ones skin.
Totally amnesic it is within.
GOD created people different shades of the earth the rainbow.
If you're black society has did it again.
If you're biracial society gives you no place,
All because of race.
Color is the covering of the soul,
Who we are, where we work, choose to live, who we love.
All races mingle with one omission back and white,
Society does not make it right.
We live in a society placarded by the color of ones skin.
Totally amnesic it is within.
Until we begin to see love has no color we'll never be free,
Of what society expects it to be.

Through These Eyes

So much corruption in all places,
Power turned greed, sexual favors and needs.
There are homeless people and acres of land where grass,
Just grows.
Wars are abundant and brewing.
Human lives taken, awakened, some granted a longer stay.
Our young become prey to the predictor.
A confidant, stranger, the next-door-neighbor.
Marriage vows broken lust given tokens to gamble with love.
What a foolish game to play.
Drive-byes has no age and guilt has no conscience.
Through these eyes I see plantations in the 2000s,
Jail cells filled with dirty laundry being dried, tried ,
By the same wash who has dirty laundry in its closets.
Agitation dissolution through these eyes I see,
Mass destruction.

Time Given

Born into imperfection,
Impervious spirit.
Placed upon solid ground.
The reward Life.
Decisions made our own.
Upright the bond.
Wrong what we all must experience and overcome.
Time a token that is endless.
Darkness surely comes and obtain the body.
Can't touch the soul.
Fighting to maintain humanity.
Murder, theft, greed, rape, cuckoldry,
Power and aversion force hate.
Time is immeasurable,
Love the categorical reality.
Pain the healer, sorrow the weakness,
Evil must be annihilated,
According to "The Law of Life".
Has been written, told, and read.

The Importance of Peace

We must demand peace and keep its control.
There's wasted money spent on the world's largest chocolate,
Easter egg and we have hungry children that need fed.
There's uncultivated land and homeless people.
Social and racial wars, world conflicts and crime,
Are abundant without solutions some resolutions.
The connection for peace is worldly hand to hand,
Land to Land.
Uniting world harmony through our voices,
Action needs to be taken, closed minds awakened,
To the importance of peace.

Run'n Child Run'n Wild

Will we ever learn?
We've walked this planet a.b.c. and a.d.c.,
In time past centuries upon centuries ago.
From love everything in exsistance was born.
Remember when you could leave your doors unlocked?
Stay out no fear, Could you do it now? Could you?
And run'n child run'n wild run child run,
Run child run.
For a child coming up in this human against human world.
Isn't slow death enough than snatching our children,

Off street corners, community parks, at school, at play,
Before and after dark, even as they kneel to pray?
Our children scream, Our children cry,
Some die, some never know.
Our children fugitives in the morning, night, run'n.
Run'n child run'n wild, run child run, run child run.
There's some animal, animals out here, taking,
Teaching, giving our babies, children weapons,
To protect, kill a skin?
Whether white, black, red, yellow, or gold,
And say they have the right to kill, steal,
Organize other animals just because of skin?
A box of crayolas has a skin, a flower,
A tree, blade of grass, prejudice has a skin.
Run child run.
As earthquakes sound in mamas' heart,
An atomic bomb set to her mind.
As nine months are washed away in bewilderment of,
Why this way?
And run'n child run'n wild, run child run.
Even dad's manhood breaks down into sobs,
Of something he can never replace, Life.
Pain, anger, madness, may make him take one,
Now he's in debt to another chattered heart,
Mama's dark and run'n child run'n wild,
Run child run, run child run,
Run for your life child. Run for your life,
Child.

I'm Different

I am different,
Glad I'm nobody else but me.
I see people of no color.
Belong to the Holy Fathers' bloodline.
Care about our young having fun,
Carrying guns.
And those that lay dead with unforgiving souls.
Don't want rains to blur my eyes with rainbows.
Streaking pass carrying deception, facades,
Condoning wrong while hiding behind smiles,
Lies.
Playing the power seekers game.
Falling in the hands of no shame.
While people get hurt to gain their fame.
Yes some find me to be strange.
Because I'm different and not the same.
Living a spiritual high on blessings.
Thankful to the One that cared to give me life.
And made me different.

Wings of Love

GOD Will...Take Care Of You

When evil conspires against you,
And times get hard.
Unbalancing setting you off guard,
Hold your head high towards the sky,
He'll hear your soul cry.

GOD Will...Take Care Of You

When tongues are sharp as a sword,
The unexpected waits to bait,
With hidden humiliation and hate,
Hold fast to your Shield of faith.
Give it to GOD and wait.
When disguises unveil seem destined to prevail,
Remember Your protector never fails.

GOD Will...Take Care Of You

Hold up your Holy Armor,
Stand tall and firm,
Battles will be learn.

One so humble, blessed,
Don't get weary, don't get stressed,
Give it to GOD and rest.
The love for GOD has pulled you through,
What you can't do he'll do for you.

GOD WILL TAKE CARE OF YOU!

Don't Cry Little Girl GODs Your Guide

Don't cry little girl wipe those tears from your eyes,
There's no need to weep.
When you're blue skies have turned gray,
Friends cast a shadow over your mind,
Turn your smile upside down.
Don't worry little girl don't frown.
When negative confronts you,
Fear jumps you, people taunt you,
And your heart feels heavy your knees get weak,
Let your heart speak.
There's no need to hide your feeling indside.
GOD knows you're bigger than that,
He's your guide.

One Judge

Only one Judge we all must answer to.
Judgement, punishment for the sake of protection?
Applause gratitude for a performance.
Laughter self-perception.
Life is not an act.
The need to achieve, produce, proceed, and fulfill,
Instructed by the Only Judge.
The Creator.

There's No Love Greater Than The Love Inside You

To love someone is to love as you love self.
There is no love greater than the love inside you.
The Creator formed you from love...HIS.

Let no man, woman, destroy your love with deception,
Or the lack of anything.
If you choose to build on a relationship,
Build it on the foundation of what you give one to another.
If one has less keeps giving less,
Is it worth to give all for less when you can be of equal?

No need for pre-fabricated dreams,
Visions of separate lifestyles when you have combined,
Your love as one.
Never give your all to a taker that has nothing to give.

Don't base your love on promises,
That materializes in words,
With no loyalty of its actions.

We strive to find inner peace inside to live,
Accordingly to the only law of life.
The Law of Love.
If we can't abide by it what do we have to offer anyone?

Nothing...

Standing In The Light

There you were,
Engulfed in a dream a moment reality,
Facing the calm to unpredicted seas,
Washing away past with no return.

There you were,
As daylight fell on unsightliness,
Night turned tears.
Smile affected by a one-time mistake,
A one night stand of ecstasy.

There you were,
Standing in the shadow alone.
Empty with the morning.
The memory of what is not meant to be.
Forgotten here you are,
Facing the calm to unpredicted seas,
Standing in the light wiser.

There's Footsteps

There are footsteps,
Early in the sometime of the morning,
Listening to only my breath,
Visions danced around in my mind.
Unkissed.
No one to console this emptyness.

The door shuts.
There are footsteps,
The "Hi babe I'm home".
Kisses of faded lipstick, smells of mixed wines,
Visions of candlelights, motel sights,
Danced in my head,
My bed left vacant.

An unsmiling smile forced back tears,
As my inner soul ripped, my heart skipped.
His heat warms untouched skin,
Thoughts of where the hell have you been?
He places a moist hand upon my breast as he rest,
Upon his face a smile of what she doesn't know.
Early in the sometime of the morning,
He hear footsteps,
The door shuts.
Forever.

He Walked Away

Storms entered his pride.
Took him aside tore at his spirit inside.
What went wrong approaches his mind?
He awaits an answer he does not find.
Misused, abused, hidden in the dark.
Daggers pierced his heart.
His soul weeped hurt came by refusing to stay.
Hate showed him its destruction.
Danger freed him.
Love showed him how to abdicate.
This inadmissible desire.
With penitence she paid he walked away.

A Tear Fell From His Eye

He heard four hi-heeled clicks.
Similar in ladylike levity,
One having a swifter pace,
The other with pomposity.
Passion and white Linen mixing,
In the air.
Scents he could ascertain the identity,
With women he knew well.
Questioning not possibly in the same place same time?
Heat reached his brow his head fell,
As her shadow turned the corner of his heart.
A tear fell from her eye.
The other angrily sighed.
A tear fell from his eye.

See Ya

How can I tell you something?
When you won't understand.
How can I trust you?
When you're not with the plan.
How can I continue to be your mate?
Tell me.

How can I share intimacy?
When you don't come home at night.
Why should I fuss or fight?
Celibacy is the course I take,
Don't know when you went fake.

Tell me.
How can I love you?
When you don't want to be loved.
How should I keep you when you don't want to stay?
How do I end this but this way?
See Ya!

She Thought

Ignominious names she was identified by.
Unconfined reverberation of others feelings, desires.
Fantasies and lies with no pride.
A taker with nothing to give in return,
For her extravagance and no class.
Income provided by the position a___.
Wanted free from the whoredoms,
Of back alleys, parked cars, inside old run down bars,
Bedrooms, storebacks, offices, waterways, and more.
Barely escaping through wives' back doors.
It all ended for awhile she became a housewife,
Chance for a change she thought.

The Paramour Game

You called me a Jezebel cause I have caramel brown skin,
Curvy hips waist thin.
Wear a black dress thigh split,
Soft pedal red painted lips.
Exposing big brown eyes with a charming smile.
Peering through your labels of deception,
As sassy, sleaze, contrary, and easy.
I'm a First Class Women need I say?
No free a__ displayed here.
No corner harlot this body not for sale.
Those pick me ups drops me offs,
A wife and other things you're trying to hide.
Second best is not my forte,
I don't play the paramour game.
You called me a Jezebel,
Because we're not the same.

Wanted

Wanted a strong man,
To hold me when I'm spineless.
To lift me when I'm strong.
Forgive me when I'm wrong.
Caress me with love pedals refresh me with love dew.
Fill emptiness with bliss,
Shower me with kisses.
Wanted a virile man conservative and keen.
Mahogany, sienna, ebony, or cream,
Esoteric aurora, sensual not callow or callous.
Protector, provider, not above any man,
Nor beneath.
Bond by love gives love to keep.
Can cry, endure pain, pick up and carry on.
Fortify his life continue to build self-esteem.
Wanted a man striving for the best.

For Some Reason

For some reason,
Combined feelings you've kept.
Guaranteed by the union you made,
To be secured in thoughts, memories,
Of a past you can never relive.

Yet you stayed and grasp on to dreams,
Of maybe, one day, that never materializes.
Caught up in lustful bliss,
Beneath all flesh contains the soul, mind, and heart.
Not aspiration of desires, not the need of,
Love.

For some reason,
Your patient wears thin,
Here you go again,
Back to the same thing.
Smoldered by the heat between your thighs,
The need to be sexually satisfied.
Nothing left but memories and thoughts of,
This is not what you want.

For some reason,
Ears that heard more eyes that seen much,
Know this is not love and for some reason you stayed.

Gave Love

Gave love .
In weakness shared.
Confusion bared.
Stress, strain, pain,
Gave love.
Showed doubt kept his love sealed,
For someone else, not even a goodbye.
Hurt carved heart,
Love hidden in the dark,
Soul felt deception.
Lies will not trip me,
Men will not flaunt me,
And this love turned bad won't hurt me again.
See,
Gave love as you played love with someone else.
Left me empty and these unsightly eyes are,
Awakened to a love not missed.

1974 Love

First peak of dawn describes his ebullience.
A love inscribed in my heart.
Twenty-five years have past with memories.
Still resplendent pictures dance through my mind.
Of his sereneness,
Arguments there were none,
Disagreements came left as quickly.
Through sickness, hardships, struggles, troubles,
We shared together.
Lonesomeness had no place.
In the threshold of love we stood.
Time split us apart sent us separate ways.
His love retained in my heart for a lifetime,
My 1974 Love.

Because I Know Him

Just because I know him,
Doesn't mean he has to be my man.
Don't need to sleep with someone I consider,
A friend.
Late nights he came to you,
Speaking of me?
They were good things honest and free.
Right things friends say and do,
Lying between the sheets is not one I choose.
Friends share in laughter each other's grief, pain,
Not all friendships are the same.
I could of maybe would of done what?
There's no evil moment nice the next.
Knowing you two are together,
Doesn't raise any heat under my dress to stoop so low.
A friend is someone, whom can comfort you in sorrow,
Share with you joy.
Make happiness a daily presence seen or heard.
If we were friends and then lovers,
A choice would be made.
We chose to be friends instead of lovers.
You're upset just because I know him.

Ms Menopause

Ms menopause address her anyway you wish.
She is heat slowly rising introducing her arrival.
Bringing dessert heat with the blanket of the sun.
Melting pot of hot flashes and million tiny pebbles,
Of sweat trickling down foreheads, and backs,
Wet cold against subsiding flames.
Leaving a cool breeze to remind us,
Ms Menopause was here will return unannounced.
Mood swings in and out.
Her entrance has brought disasters,
She does not need a welcome mat,
Nor approval, she visits briefly, sometimes stays,
For a while.
When she surpasses with no return,
Only her race of aging lingers.

Could Be Dreaming

Could be dreaming please don't wake me, shake me,
Rattle or roll me,
Leave me be.
The love that molded me holds me,
Teaches me, scolds me.
Lets me know when I'm wrong, right, or failed.
Presence always near.
Pain, Sorrow, Joy, are my companions.
The Power that controls me protects me.
The spirit within is His gift Life.
Could be dreaming but I'm not.

The Comedian

Is it funny when jokes don't bring laughter?
Cries no tears.
Isn't funny,
Cutting words to slash intentionally,
No reason. See you just,
Can't take the fool out of some.
Isn't it funny how far some will go?
To impress themselves?

Isn't it funny how desire,
Uproot exultation?
Flaunts humiliation with pride.
It isn't funny to play with feelings.

Is it funny when accusations,
Shows ignorance falls prey to insecurity?
Some feel no need to change.
Kindness no milksop to weakness.
Hurt no battle for pain.
It isn't funny how some speculate chances.

Is it funny when age is thrown as a factor?
Abuse misuse ?
Naiveté ripped of its maidenhead?
Lay dead?
It isn't funny to cast aside inner beauty,
Trip forethought unknown.
Punster some may be.
See.
It isn't funny.

My Best Friend and Me

Dedicated to Lynn Johnson

She sat at my feet,
Railroad Mill Snuff in her hand.
Talked of the fight between my best friend and me.
Why what happened shouldn't be.
She took her last breath of air and died.
Earthquakes erupted in my mind,
Wish I could turn back time.
Emptiness enter my being,
My soul weep my world turned upside down.
Darkness clouded my eyes with tears.
Awakened my fears.
No one's fault I was told she was tired and old.
A strong woman full of grace,
God took her to His special place.
Spirit free part of her inside of me.
We treasure her love eternally.
My best friend and me.

Reality

Reattach Me To Your Vine

My life belongs to you LORD.
The road I travel is too wide,
A place where self understanding can't hide.
Through passing storms of life,
The turbulence of sin is a battle I can't win.
Nor can be kept within.
Words have no meaning and eyes seeing the pain,
Not ending.
Baring a cross too heavy for these weakened shoulders.
Sleepless nights into daylight strife,
You won the battle I try to fight.
Forgive me LORD,
For forsaking you again,
Your peace I can not find,
Help me to root,
Reattached me to your Vine.

Youngblood

Youngblood was young, strong, and free.
Mind filled with facades.
Youngblood grew up with anger, rage,
Drinking, smoking, under age.
Afraid to cry lived a lie.
Thought he was too tough to die.
Youngblood had no ones' support,
 No one seem to care, or shared his life of confusion,
Pain.
Youngblood took life as a game.
Stealing, killing became his fame.
Branded by society he felt strong and free.
A lifestyle he thought he won.
His life was snatched by another's gun.
Society had won.

Bad Boys

In jail cells doing time for the title "Crime."
Bad Boys, buy, sell, and have inside informants, outside,
Traps.
Used good people, bad guys, some on crac.
Bad Boys are all the Bad Boys, whom are there to protect,
Each other as innocent blood flow, egos.
Bad boys don't care.
Bad Boys tear down communities, families.
Take lives as a game.
Bad Boys hurt for fortune and fame.
The soul is within and there are Bad Souls.

Back In The Day When?

Hip-hop was the play.
Be-bop a forte.
Groups gathered in their basements,
With drums, lead guitar, bass, and horn.
Piercing the air with heads bobbin people talk'n.
Walk'n, stop'n, look'n to see who is blowing,
That funky horn, that was back in the day.
Sitting on street corners, bust heads, kids,
The elderly, and those nosey women,
Peeking through curtains, slowly opening hallway doors,
Running to get a cup to put up against the wall.
Back in the day.
Grumpy old men, wino men, fresh old men, and young men.
Children play'n everywhere eyes upon them,
Now it's community watch.
Yet no one sees or those that do keep silent.
Do something wrong your mom or dad was called.
Couple of minutes their in your face.
Yet our children are snatched, offended, and raped.
The elderly prize jewels, helping them with groceries,
Crossing the street, shoveled their walkways, took them to church.
They were safe yet our elderly are beaten, offended, and raped.
Back in the day people cared.

Mamma Knew

Extension cords, rope, and so many household items,
Mamma threw.
Catch us doing something, anything wrong,
Snatch a few branches off a tree.
Lights shining brightly against awakening eyes,
It's five o'clock in the morning wake up call.
Either by the rooster or the smell of an old fashion,
Hearty breakfast.
Mamma knew.
Sunday mornings off you go to Sunday school.
Long sit in church, shifting from side to side,
Listening to Gods' messenger, church rock'n of real hometown,
Folk gathered together in spiritual harmony.
Mamma said,
You pot smok'n, laid back non talk'n,
Raise your hand to smack this face.
You'll be a runner that never wins.
Still have your daddy's grin.
Just you and I.
Boy wipe those tears from your eyes!

Mamma cared, shared her love, she seen too many,
Neglected children struggling young mothers,
Cracked out brothers uneducated, violated,
Suspended rage, jobless and more.
Mamma did what she had to do for,
Her children, grand children, great grandchildren,
That she adored.
Mamma knew she had God's love.

GOD Will Set You Free

Years have past by and the fight still,
Burns in your heart.
Fighting a battle behind bars that even cages,
The truth you hold.
No one listen to the story you told.
Preparing for freedom that may never be?
You're a warrior they can't see.
Blocks. blunders, interruptions, corruption,
Distortion hinders your way.
Keep your sanity day by day they can't snatch that away.
When night falls no one hears your soul cry.
No one answers your questions why.
Another day unfolds trying to get the story told.
You're a warrior they can't see.
God will set you free.
Keep fighting, keep striving, and don't get weak and cold,
You may loose your youth but there's grace,
In growing old.
When you feel there's no fight left,
Give it to God and rest.
You only faced with what you can bare.
May seem wrong even unfair.
Preparing for freedom that may never be?
GOD will be the one that will set you free.

Setback Backing Back

That brother, dude, homeboy, is a setback.
Backed his own back against life.
Now its "Yo bro, hey daddy, what's up roadie,
Got a dime on some wine?
Crac blow'n his mind shortening his time,
The white crystal ghost, gold chains,
Fancy cars, jump'n in out of bars,
Corner pimps pimp'n minds turning them into drug zombies.
Transporting drugs gonna do time in time,
Behind metal bars maybe again.
Another setback chained against life,
Who will release him set him free?
From other setbacks who keep backing back,
Against life.

Crac

Crac disguises the need it feels.
Hiding behind a sunlit smile filled with lies, truth.
Convincing self of lost will.
Substance power insist upon tainted lifestyles,
In addition facades of illusory.
Crac sold your soul,
That is already filled with future death.
Crac lied to your mother.
Stole from your brothers,
Used good women, men, taking lives,
Giving false hope false love,
To buy and give to others who live in the same arena.
The bait those who share in its life of facades.
Integument the addiction that leaves you trapped,
Crac sold your soul.
Can't get it back.

Spirits Free Wings of Love Reality of God's Love

Soaring through life on the <u>Wings of Love</u>.
Guided by light through darkness,
Pathways narrow and unstraight.
<u>Spirits Free</u>.

Life and time are unpredictable,
Everyday lived is a joy of the beautifulest gift,
The <u>Reality</u> of <u>GOD's Love</u>.

Come Inside

Conclusion

This is a part of my life lived and the eyes that seen the words to write and give back my expressions, opinions, thoughts, visions, and views of my human experience.

Thank you for Coming Inside.

Come inside

I'd like to order_____(number of copies)

I've enclosed_____($14.95 per book + 5.95 shipping and handling)

Send Order Form To:

Harobed Publishing Creations
P.O. Box 8195
Pittsburgh, PA 15217-0195

I'd like a personally autographed copy signed to:

_____my_____(relationship to you)

Send my copy of **COME INSIDE** to:

name_____

address_____

city_____state_____zip_____

Please allow 2 weeks for delivery of your order

If oders are 500 or more please contact:
Ada Small at 412-243-9299